D1124181

DATE DUE

OCT 15 1996			
OCT 29			
NOV 1 9 1996			
JUL 2 4 1997			

FIRST LOOK

UNDER THE GROUND

For a free color catalog describing Gareth Stevens' list of high-quality children's books, call 1-800-341-3569 (USA) or 1-800-461-9120 (Canada).

Library of Congress Cataloging-in-Publication Data

Butler, Daphne, 1945-
  [Under the ground]
  First look under the ground / Daphne Butler.
    p. cm. -- (First look)
  Previously published as: Under the ground. c1990.
  Includes bibliographical references and index.
  Summary: A simple introduction to what can be found naturally underground and what people have put there.
  ISBN 0-8368-0507-0
  1. Underground construction--Juvenile literature. [1. Geology. 2. Underground construction.] I. Title. II. Series: Butler, Daphne, 1945- First look.
TA712.B87 1991
550--dc20   90-10245

North American edition first published in 1991 by

Gareth Stevens Children's Books
1555 North RiverCenter Drive, Suite 201
Milwaukee, Wisconsin 53212, USA

Photograph credits: Cheddar Showcaves, Cheddar Gorge, cover, 10; ZEFA, all others.

Series editor: Rita Reitci
Design: M&M Design Partnership
Cover design: Laurie Shock

Printed in the United States of America

1 2 3 4 5 6 7 8 9 97 96 95 94 93 92 91

FIRST LOOK

DAPHNE BUTLER

UNDER THE GROUND

Gareth Stevens Children's Books
MILWAUKEE

Books in the
FIRST LOOK series:

CONTENTS

GROUND IS USUALLY HARD

Look at the ground around you. What is it made of? Concrete? Grass? Dirt?

If you jump on the ground, you'll find that it's usually very hard. What do you think is under the ground that makes it so hard?

LAYERS OF ROCK

These cliffs are made of layer upon layer of rock.
Under the ground lie layers of rock just like these.

Our home, the planet Earth, is a huge ball of rock
that is billions of years old.

10

OPENINGS IN ROCK

Sometimes rock has large openings inside called caves. Have you ever been inside a cave?

Water has been dripping into these caves for a very long time. Can you see what has happened to the rock?

LIVING IN CAVES

Thousands of years ago, people lived in caves. Would you like to live in a cave?

Cave people painted pictures on the walls. These pictures are still there to tell us about the lives of these people.

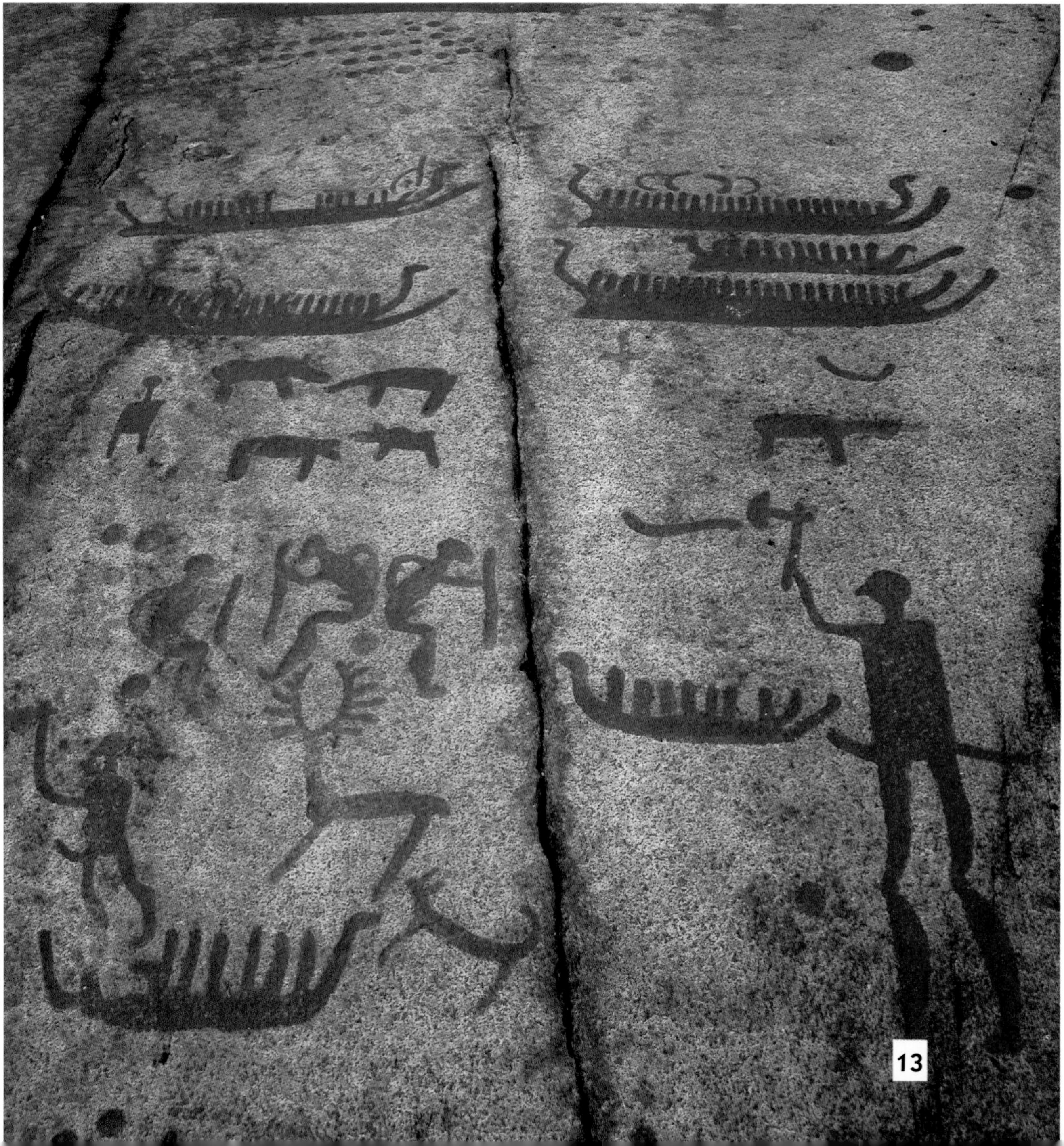

13

HIDDEN UNDER THE GROUND

Dinosaurs lived on Earth millions of years ago, long before there were any people.

A dinosaur left this footprint in mud. Over the years, the mud slowly turned into rock.

15

DIGGING FOR COAL

Coal is much older than dinosaurs.

Long ago, huge ferns and trees grew on the Earth. When they died, they fell into water and were covered with mud. Long, long afterward, they turned into coal.

Why do we dig for coal? What do we use it for?

17

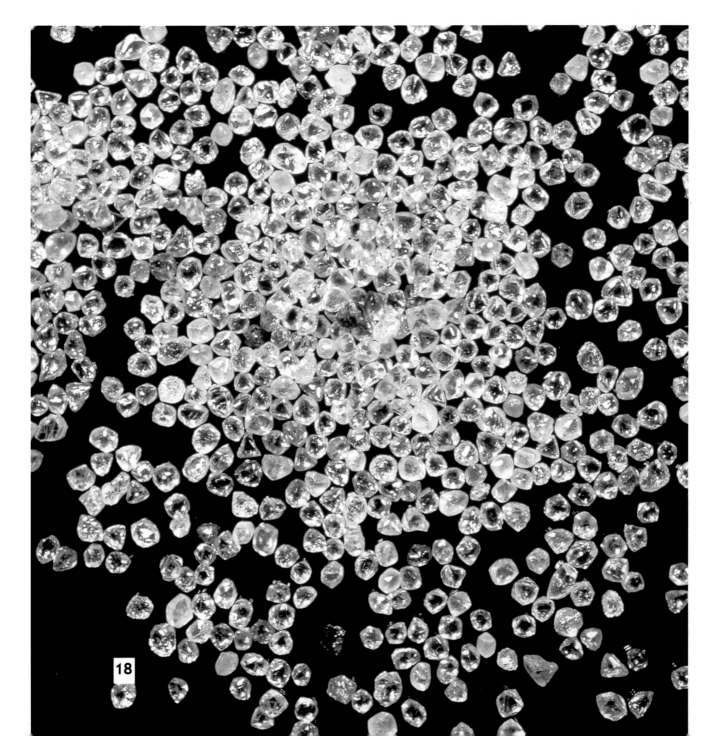

DIAMONDS SPARKLE

Not all rocks are dull gray or brown. Some are much brighter. Diamonds are clear, sparkling stones that are very hard.

What can diamonds be used for?

TUNNELS UNDER THE GROUND

People dig tunnels to find coal and diamonds.
They also dig tunnels to build railroads and roads
under the ground.

Have you ever been in a tunnel underground?
Can you remember what it was like?

21

MAKING TRENCHES

Workers often bury pipes under the ground. A backhoe makes a long trench for the pipes and later covers them with soil.

These pipes will carry water. Can you think of anything else that goes in pipes under the ground?

ANIMALS THAT DIG

Many animals make safe homes under the ground. Here are two. Can you think of others?

Look at the roots in the soil. Plants get water and food from the soil through their roots.

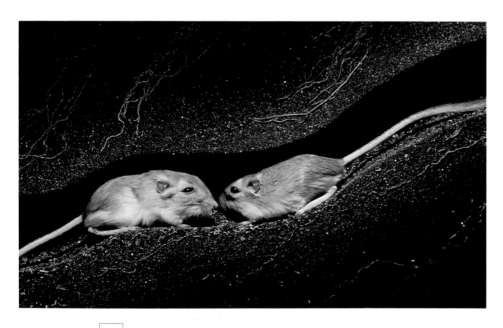

25

WHAT IS SOIL?

Soil is made of grains of rock mixed with the tiny remains of dead plants and animals.

Wind, rain, and frost break the rock into tiny grains. It takes a long, long time to make soil.

27

NEW ROCK FROM UNDER THE GROUND

This volcano is smoking and steaming as it brings ash and melted rock up from under the ground. When these cool, they will form new rock.

Only some parts of the world have volcanoes. Do you know of any?

More Books about under the Ground

Animals That Burrow. Morris (Raintree)
Animals Underground. Ruffault (Young Discovery Library)
Caves. Gans (Harper & Row Junior Books)
Dinosaurs Walked Here and Other Stories Fossils Tell. Lauber (Bradbury)
A First Look at Rocks. Selsam (Walker)
From Dinosaurs to Fossils. Fuchshuber (Carolrhoda)
From Swamp to Coal. Mitgutsch (Carolrhoda)
Gemstones. Mercer (Gloucester Press/Franklin Watts)
In Coal Country. Hendershot (Knopf)
Rocks and Minerals. Podendorf (Childrens Press)
Soil. Webb (Franklin Watts)
Tunnels. Gibbons (Holiday)
Tunnels. Rickard (Bookwright/Franklin Watts)
Under the Ground. Booth (Raintree)
Underground Life. Roberts (Childrens Press)

Glossary

Cave: A natural opening in the Earth that has an entrance. Underground water can wear away soft stone to make a cave. Water dripping into the cave can leave behind deposits of stone in strange shapes. Sea caves are made by waves pounding against cliffs.

Coal: A natural black solid that burns. It comes from trees and other plants that died and were buried for millions of years. Coal is a fuel used for heating. It is also used to make electricity, gas, and chemicals. We find coal under the ground in layers called seams.

Concrete: A mixture of water, sand, gravel, and cement. The cement is made out of clay and burned lime. When the concrete dries, it becomes as hard as stone. Concrete is used in making buildings, bridges, walks, and roads.

Diamonds: Crystals formed deep inside the earth, most likely in volcanoes. Diamonds are the hardest known material. The prettiest diamonds are used as gems. But most diamonds and diamond dust are used for grinding and cutting tools in industry.

Dinosaurs: A branch of reptiles that came into being 225 million years ago. Some dinosaurs were the largest and fiercest animals that ever lived. They ruled life on Earth until they died out 65 million years ago. The word *dinosaur* means "terrible lizard."

Planet: A body in space that moves around a star. Our Sun is a star. Nine planets travel around the Sun, each on its own path. Earth is one of them. A star makes its own heat, but a planet does not. A planet is cold unless it is warmed by the heat of a star.

Volcano: An opening in the Earth's surface through which ash, melted rock, gas, and steam are forced out from deep inside. The ash and melted rock form a cone around the opening.

Index

A number that is in **boldface** type means that the page has a picture of the subject on it.